IF FOUND PI

👤 _____

✉ _____

📱 _____

Greater Than a Tourist Book Series
Reviews from Readers

I think the series is wonderful and beneficial for tourists to get information before visiting the city.

-Seckin Zumbul, Izmir Turkey

I am a world traveler who has read many trip guides but this one really made a difference for me. I would call it a heartfelt creation of a local guide expert instead of just a guide.

-Susy, Isla Holbox, Mexico

New to the area like me, this is a must have!

-Joe, Bloomington, USA

This is a good series that gets down to it when looking for things to do at your destination without having to read a novel for just a few ideas.

-Rachel, Monterey, USA

Good information to have to plan my trip to this destination.

-Pennie Farrell, Mexico

Great ideas for a port day.

-Mary Martin USA

Aptly titled, you won't just be a tourist after reading this book. You'll be greater than a tourist!

-Alan Warner, Grand Rapids, USA

Even though I only have three days to spend in San Miguel in an upcoming visit, I will use the author's suggestions to guide some of my time there. An easy read - with chapters named to guide me in directions I want to go.

 -Robert Catapano, USA

Great insights from a local perspective! Useful information and a very good value!

 -Sarah, USA

This series provides an in-depth experience through the eyes of a local. Reading these series will help you to travel the city in with confidence and it'll make your journey a unique one.

-Andrew Teoh, Ipoh, Malaysia

>TOURIST

GREATER THAN A TOURIST- HYDRA ISLAND ATTICA GREECE

50 Travel Tips from a Local

Caroline Walter

Greater Than a Tourist- Hydra, Attica, Greece Copyright © 2019 by CZYK Publishing LLC. All Rights Reserved.

All rights reserved. No part of this book may be reproduced in any form or by any electronic or mechanical means including information storage and retrieval systems, without permission in writing from the author. The only exception is by a reviewer, who may quote short excerpts in a review.

The statements in this book are of the authors and may not be the views of CZYK Publishing or Greater Than a Tourist.

Cover designed by: Ivana Stamenkovic
Cover Image by author.

CZYK Publishing Since 2011.

Greater Than a Tourist
Visit our website at GreaterThanaTourist.com

Lock Haven, PA
All rights reserved.

ISBN: 9781091889187

>TOURIST
50 TRAVEL TIPS FROM A LOCAL

\>TOURIST

BOOK DESCRIPTION

Are you excited about planning your next trip?

Do you want to try something new?

Would you like some guidance from a local?

If you answered yes to any of these questions, then this Greater Than a Tourist book is for you.

Greater Than a Tourist- Hydra, Attica, Greece by Caroline Walter offers the inside scoop on Hydra. Most travel books tell you how to travel like a tourist. Although there is nothing wrong with that, as part of the Greater Than a Tourist series, this book will give you travel tips from someone who has lived at your next travel destination.

In these pages, you will discover advice that will help you throughout your stay. This book will not tell you exact addresses or store hours but instead will give you excitement and knowledge from a local that you may not find in other smaller print travel books.

Travel like a local. Slow down, stay in one place, and get to know the people and culture. By the time you finish this book, you will be eager and prepared to travel to your next destination.

Inside this travel guide book you will find:

- Insider tips from a local.

- Bonus tips *50 Things to Know About Packing Light for Travel* by bestselling author Manidipa Bhattacharyya.

- Packing and planning list.

- List of travel questions to ask yourself or others while traveling.

- A place to write your travel bucket list.

OUR STORY

Traveling is a passion of the "Greater than a Tourist" series creator. Lisa studied abroad in college, and for their honeymoon Lisa and her husband toured Europe. During her travels to Malta, an older man tried to give her some advice based on his own experience living on the island since he was a young boy. She was not sure if she should talk to the stranger but was interested in his advice. When traveling to some places she was wary to talk to locals because she was afraid that they weren't being genuine. Through her travels, Lisa learned how much locals had to share with tourists. Lisa created the *Greater Than a Tourist* book series to help connect people with locals. A topic that locals are very passionate about sharing.

TABLE OF CONTENTS

BOOK DESCRIPTION
Our Story
TABLE OF CONTENTS
DEDICATION
ABOUT THE AUTHOR
HOW TO USE THIS BOOK
FROM THE PUBLISHER
WELCOME TO
> TOURIST
1. How To Get There
2. How To Get Around
3. A Paradise For Families
4. A Paradise For Nature Lovers
5. A Paradise For Sportsmen
6. A Paradise for Cat Lovers
7. A Paradise for Fishermen
8. A Paradise For History Lovers
9. A Paradise For Painters
10. A Perfect Place For A Wedding
11. Best Places To Stay: Budget
12. Best Places To Stay: Medium-priced
13. Best Places To Stay: Luxury
14. Best Places To Eat Like A Local
15. Best Places To Try Fusion Food

16. Best Coffee In Town
17. Best Cocktails in Town
18. Amygdalota: The Local Delicacy
19. Horta: The Greens From The Hills
20. Other Villages To Explore
21. Best Beach For Children
22. Best Beach For Swimming
23. Best Beach To Meet Young Locals
24. Best Beach For Older People
25. Go Scuba Diving
26. Sunset Cruise
27. Feel The Nostalgic Atmosphere
28. Orthodox Easter In Hydra
29. Independence Day In Hydra
30. Miaoulis Festival
31. Carnival Season In Hydra
32. Zourva Monastery Celebrations
33. Climb To The Top Of Mount Eros
34. Dress code
35. Take A Greek Language Course
36. Listen To Greek Music Through Summer
37. Listen To Bouzouki Live Music
38. Experience The Rebetiko Festival
39. Join Leonard Cohen's Fans
40. Local Favourite Foods To Try
41. Local Nightlife

\>TOURIST

42. St Constantine's Festival
43. How Much To Tip
44. Bites And Other Issues
45. Safety or Health Concerns
46. It's All-Greek To Me
47. Time For Shopping
48. Before You Leave
49. Take A Boat To The Next Island
50. Buy A House

TOP REASONS TO BOOK THIS TRIP

Other Resources:

50 THINGS TO KNOW ABOUT PACKING LIGHT FOR TRAVEL

Packing and Planning Tips

Travel Questions

Travel Bucket List

NOTES

DEDICATION

This book is dedicated to Leonard Cohen and its songs, some of them written on this island! To Marianne and Suzanne, whom I had the opportunity to meet while living here.

\>TOURIST

ABOUT THE AUTHOR

Caroline Walter is a 41 year-old French woman, who lives on Hydra Island. Caroline loves to learn new languages, travel the Greek Islands, and taste local delicacies.

Caroline enjoys travelling to both mainland Greece and other islands, such as Spetses, Naxos or Crete.

She has spent 15 years on the Greek island of Hydra, and has learnt some Modern Greek, through meeting with the locals. Her passions are ceramic making, crafts and painting.

HOW TO USE THIS BOOK

The *Greater Than a Tourist* book series was written by someone who has lived in an area for over three months. The goal of this book is to help travelers either dream or experience different locations by providing opinions from a local. The author has made suggestions based on their own experiences. Please check before traveling to the area in case the suggested places are unavailable.

Travel Advisories: As a first step in planning any trip abroad, check the Travel Advisories for your intended destination.
https://travel.state.gov/content/travel/en/traveladvisories/traveladvisories.html

FROM THE PUBLISHER

Traveling can be one of the most important parts of a person's life. The anticipation and memories that you have are some of the best. As a publisher of the Greater Than a Tourist book series, as well as the popular *50 Things to Know* book series, we strive to help you learn about new places, spark your imagination, and inspire you. Wherever you are and whatever you do I wish you safe, fun, and inspiring travel.

Lisa Rusczyk Ed. D.
CZYK Publishing

>TOURIST

WELCOME TO
> TOURIST

>TOURIST

*"I live on a hill, and life has
been going on here exactly the
same for hundreds of years"*

Leonard Cohen,

The typical tourist guide sometimes overviews Hydra, in Greek "Ydra", as a small rocky island in the Argo-saronic archipelago, packing it in a one-day visit tour. Once you are familiar with locals though, its historic fame, its architecture and its natural beauties can fill your whole holiday in Greece! Hydra counts around 3 000 inhabitants, but in the summer time, this number can double. Villages on the islands are located on the front side of the island, while the back of the island is wild. There are no major roads crossing the island. It has stayed hundred years the same, while being so close to Athens, the capital city. It is famous around Greece for its history and cultural heritage.

1. HOW TO GET THERE

You can get to Hydra only by sea, or, like the jet set, by helicopter. By sea, you can catch a ferry of the Hellenic Seaways Company, called "Flying Cat" in

Piraeus Port, and it takes approximately 2 hours to get there. In winter months, you may have to check the weather forecast in advance, for storms and possible wind conditions. If you are travelling from Greece mainland, you can also catch a shuttle boat from the village "Metoxi". This crossing takes around 20 minutes, and operates on the hour.

http://www.hydralines.gr/routes/
https://hellenicseaways.gr

2. HOW TO GET AROUND

Once you set foot on Hydra, forget about cars, bicycles, Vespa, Lime or Bird scooters! Hydra is one of the few islands in the world totally preserved! Everywhere you go, you will walk, use a donkey, or catch a small sea taxi boat. It is ideal to make you feel close to nature, relax, and exercise. There are many maps available at local shops, pick one up, and put your walking shoes on.

3. A PARADISE FOR FAMILIES

Hydra welcomes all types of tourists, from the group of Greek students celebrating summer, to

Hollywood celebrities. The fact that it is car-free makes it a perfect spot for families with small children. Families will find peace of mind, and children will find plenty of play companions in the local public gardens, taverns and small pebble beaches. The locals worship children of all nationalities, and language barriers are forgotten easily.

4. A PARADISE FOR NATURE LOVERS

If you can travel to Hydra in springtime, wild flowers will welcome you as you walk out of the boat. Poppies, daisies, iris, and green hills as if you were in Ireland. Most tourists imagine Greece as a summer destination. However, spring is one of the best times to visit Hydra. Temperatures are still cool enough (around 20 degrees Celsius) giving hikers & runners an opportunity to explore the hiking tracks around the island.

5. A PARADISE FOR SPORTSMEN

Hiking, running, swimming, horse riding, soccer, tennis, kickboxing, Greek dancing…these activities are alive on Hydra island. Early April, every year, a mountain race competition takes place, bringing many visitors to the island. Runners climb to the top of Mt Ilias, and come back down through fields and woods. In November, a "swim-run" event also takes place on the island. Both Greek and international sportsmen participate.

6. A PARADISE FOR CAT LOVERS

Many international television programs filmed documentaries in Hydra, with regards to wild cats. Wild cats are everywhere. We once meet a lady photographer from the National Geographic, visiting Hydra for a short day trip. She finally returned and spent months here, shooting every cat, as she used to photograph lions in Africa for the famous magazine. She now returns every year, and became a fundraiser for the animals. I also had the opportunity to meet the

>TOURIST

National Japanese TV crew, while they filmed a documentary on cats. Hydra is definitely a cosmopolitan island!

7. A PARADISE FOR FISHERMEN

A few years ago, some locals started to rent small boats to tourists, but they also take them on their traditional wooden boats, providing day trips fishing with them. In the autumn months, from late September, to mid-November, local fishermen take pride in catching the local "calamari" (octopus/squid).

8. A PARADISE FOR HISTORY LOVERS

Hydra gave birth to a few famous politicians, Prime Ministers, but also to the revolutionary leaders that freed Greece from Turkish invasion, during the 1821 Independence war. There are two major museums to visit while you are here: the Koundouriotis Mansion, and the National Archives, with local costumes, paintings, and also relics such as Navy leader Andreas Miaouli's Heart.

You can do a walking tour with Maria, for example, to discover specific details of the island, in English.

(A link to her website: http://hydrawalkingtours.com)

9. A PARADISE FOR PAINTERS

Hydra is simply a painting in real life! Wherever you look, every detail is worth a sketch. From its untouched architectural style, to the seaside, the Ministry of Archaeology preserved every detail. There are no high-rise buildings. Local carpenters still craft the doors and windows of all houses with wood. Flora and fauna make perfect subjects for any painters. From the wild cat, to the local donkey, there are many inspiring contents on Hydra for painters. Likewise, many locals became famous painters, not only in Hydra, but worldwide. To mention only one master, I would recommend that you visit his house, Panayiotis Tetsis, now deceased. Modern painters living on Hydra include Dimitri Fatouros, Tom

Powell, and Michael Lawrence. It is possible to meet them, or visit their workshop.

> *"Aesthetically it is perfect"*
>
> Henry Miller about Hydra

10. A PERFECT PLACE FOR A WEDDING

Many Greeks people from Athens come to Hydra for their wedding. There are amazing spots near by the waterfront, and in other small villages to make the event a perfect memory. When you visit the island on a weekend, you may find yourself among the guests. Sometimes the bride & groom use the local transport (donkey) to get to the small churches, other times, they board on a wooden "caiqui" (boat), to reach further away churches.

11. BEST PLACES TO STAY: BUDGET

Hydra used to be a paradise for backpackers, in the 1970s. Nowadays, it may be described as a little off budget for backpackers. For example, compared with other Greek islands, there are no youth hostels here. Also camping is not an option. However, there are some budget accommodation options. Among those, I would recommend the Glaros Guesthouse (it is conveniently located on the harbour side, and inexpensive). Another safe choice is Efi Pension, near the church clock tower. It has two lovely rooms with balconies, with view over the port. Also not far from the main harbour are the Botsis Pension, and Erofili Pension. These are all Greek family owned pensions, and less expensive than most AirBnB type of rooms you may find.

12. BEST PLACES TO STAY: MEDIUM-PRICED

If your budget is slightly higher, you may want to check out the Hippocampus Hotel, with its beautiful indoor garden, and double room with sea view terrace. Also the Orloff Hotel, which describes itself as "Echoes of Nostalgia" is a typical Hydriot style mansion, renovated, with an indoor garden and lemon trees. Both places offer great breakfast, with Hydra handmade cakes, jams and honey.

13. BEST PLACES TO STAY: LUXURY

Finally, if you are willing to splash it all, there are plenty of choices for a luxury stay. My favourite places, based on their location, and staff, are the following:

The Four Seasons villas and bungalows, Vlychos: these are located right on Plakes beach, within olive tree groves. There are no motor vehicles around, only the sound of the sea, and birds! The hotel has its own private motorboat to shuttle you from the main Hydra harbour to the little village of Vlychos. It also houses a tasty tavern and coffee place.

Hydra Hotel: this is a renovated luxury "arxontiko" mansion, with high ceilings, and panoramic views over the harbour. This hotel is best for people who handle steps well, as you need to walk up and climb quite a few stairs to get to it. But the view and the welcome are worth it!

Bratsera Hotel: located just five minutes from the boat decking spot, this former sponge factory is an intimate, yet, luxurious hotel. It is the only one with an indoor swimming pool, and no steps to access.

It is a favourite among celebrities, but also a gathering place for locals in summer time for diners near the pool.

14. BEST PLACES TO EAT LIKE A LOCAL

While in Greece, you may think that restaurants are catered only for tourists, in Hydra, you will still find the traditional taverns, with a few tables, where the recipes are told from mothers to daughters.

One of the oldest taverns on the island is Lulu, also called "Kalamaras' from the name of the owners. With its turquoise walls and chairs, it seems timeless. Greek-American visitors still come to see where they used to dance "Hasapiko". At Lulu's you can try the traditional homemade dishes, such as Pastichio, Moussaka, Calamari, Fava, Kokkinisto (Beef meat in red sauce). All of these come in at a reasonable price, and friendly hospitality. It is not fancy, but it is the atmosphere that counts.

Another long-standing local tavern is "Anita", from the owner name. Both her brother and husbands were fishermen, so this is the right place to try a seafood dish, if you like those. In summer time, it is buzzling with tourists too, but it is a local's hangout, as soon as there is a special occasion, such as baptism, name day or anniversary.

If you fancy getting out of the main village, try walking to "Mandraki" bay, around 30 minutes by foot, to the right of the boat arrival. There, you will find the tavern "Lazarus" as it is called by the locals, or "Mandraki 1800". Its blue chairs, white tables on the terrace that dominates the pebble beach, are mostly filled with local sailors. In summer months, Greek from Athens, who own houses on Hydra, also come to this tiny place to have seafood, between swims. You may not find a seat, especially on Sundays, but if you can, do stop!

15. BEST PLACES TO TRY FUSION FOOD

Since 2015, various places opened, bringing "fusion Greek food" tastes to Hydra. If you are staying around the harbour side, you may try the "Omilos" seafront restaurant. This is a modern, sleek, fusion food place, which opened in the former "Lagoudera" building. While it is open for lunch with a reasonably priced set menu, the best time to go is for sunset. The main terrace overlooks the waves, and you will be able to taste fine seafood or meat dishes, while admiring the sun setting behind the Peloponnese hills across from Hydra. Prices for diner are quite high, compared to other places in town.

Another newly opened fusion restaurant is "Techné", near the Avlaki cove. To get there, you will need to walk up the hill round the harbour for another 15 minutes. This former nightclub in the 1980s re-opened a few years ago, after being totally renovated. The young chef, Greek of origin, first worked in London, and then, decided to take his chance on an island. It is now fully packed every summer night, and you definitely will need a booking to come and experience it.

16. BEST COFFEE IN TOWN

I am an addict to coffee! Mostly I fell for espresso and cappuccinos, and I cannot resist one from the Pirate bar. It is facing the harbour, and keep its quality of coffee to the top. Other places in town are available, but if you are a keen coffee-drinker, I believe the Pirate will fulfil your wishes. For Greek coffees, the best place to sit would be "Hydra's corner" near the Alpha Bank building. It is a local hangout too, and from there, you can have a filled morning, watching the world goes by. From donkey men waiting for luggage, to the latest trendy students, this coffee shop offers a friendly service, and a mixed crowd.

17. BEST COCKTAILS IN TOWN

Personally, the very best place in Hydra, and in Greece, to have cocktail, with a one of a kind view, is "Hydronetta" bar. A long-time favourite of locals and tourists alike, it comes to live from April to October. While in the morning you can taste Greek yogurt and breakfast there, the best hour is "Happy Hour" for sunset. With its tables and chairs facing the sea, Dokos and Spestes islands, and the Peloponnese hills, you can see the sun goes down in the Mediterranean while listening to the best music, and sip any cocktail of your choice. Service is always friendly, professional, and with a good pricing.

The Pirate Bar, formerly owned by Menelaus "the Pirate" it is now a local favourite, with owners Takis & Wendy. You can have brunch, lunch, or cocktails here, depending on the hour. Many Greek locals sailors, fishermen, but also celebrities come here, for its atmosphere & warm welcome.

18. AMYGDALOTA: THE LOCAL DELICACY

From the word "amygdalo" in Greek, which means "almonds", the amygdalotas of Hydra are famous all around Greece. These sweet almonds macaroons are unique to the island, and to the shop "Tsangaris". Located in a small lane off the main harbour, the recipe came from great grand mothers, and is still secretly kept by the great grand son. Another bakery shop on the island also serves this delicacy. You can try them also at Flora's Anemone bakery.

19. HORTA: THE GREENS FROM THE HILLS

I had a chance to meet "Kiria Danae" (Ms Danae) an 90 year-old lady with bright white hair, the first few months I moved on Hydra. As I used to live 30 minutes from the town centre, on the hills, I usually met her on my way to town. She would go up the steps and collect "Horta", a mix of greens that the older locals know. "Horta" is rinsed, boiled and served usually with fish dishes, or by itself with lemon juice. It is said to keep you in good health! Taste wise: it is a bit of an acquired taste. You may find it bitter. However, it is surely a dish to try while you are on Hydra.

20. OTHER VILLAGES TO EXPLORE

While Hydra is both the name of the island and the main village's name, there are also a few other settlements, accessible by foot, or by sea taxi.

You can walk to Mandraki Beach settlement and Beach resort, within around 30 minutes. It is a 2 kilometre-walk, which is easy enough in winter, but can be hot in summer. By sea taxi, it costs around 15 euros, but you will get there in 5 minutes. In Mandraki, you can find a man-made sandy beach, a small marina, with wooden boats, a typical tavern, and some houses to rent. There are no supermarkets, nor shops, so you need to take some water along with you, when you go there.

Kamini is another village, accessible on the left side of the island. It became famous in the 1960s, for Greek visitors, through black and white movies, filmed there. Kamini is a charming fishing village, with its own personality. While in summer time, it is now filled with tourists and rented houses, in springtime, it is an exceptional place to visit. Wild flowers are everywhere! At Easter time, the tiny harbour welcomes the "Good Friday" orthodox procession. The religious icon is taken into the sea, held by 8 local men. Kamini is an easy walk if you are in good shape, but there are steps on the way. If you prefer, you can board a water taxi from the main harbour to take you there.

Finally, Vlychos is the last village to visit. By foot, it can be reached within one hour, following the seaside, while the mountain trail takes you inside the village. Vlychos is a bit abandoned during the winter months, with few people living there full time. It is mostly a summer settlement, with hotels, small Bed & Breakfast, villas to rent. There are many foreigners, mostly Italians, who became almost "locals", and have been coming there for 10 or 20 years, every year. It is an easy location to get a mix of mountain view, local food, and small coves to swim or snorkel.

>TOURIST

21. BEST BEACH FOR CHILDREN

The so-called "Baby beach" in Hydra refers to Avlaki, a small cover, down many steps inside the pine trees. There, any afternoon of summer, you will find around 10 to 20 small kids with their mums, learning how to swim. There are pebbles, no sand, and you will need to take your plastic shoes with you, to avoid a few sea urchins. However, it is fairly protected from the main waves of other swimming spots. There are no umbrellas, nor coffee shops there, so everyone take their drinks or picnic with them. You may meet new friends if you visit the cove every day, and you will be able to try some of your Greek phrases.

Mandraki Beach is another easy choice for kids to swim. This man-made sandy beach is less spectacular, but convenient. It offers a shuttle boat service from the main village, every half hour. It also has a coffee bar, with fruit salads, ice creams, juices and light meals. A positive point is the shower service available to everyone and the toilets, where you can change. It gathers a crowd of local Greek families, with young children. There are no waves, and no sea urchins.

22. BEST BEACH FOR SWIMMING

A favourite swim spot for tourists and locals is St Nicolas Beach. It is located at the back of the island, in an area that you can access only by boat. There are shuttle boats travelling from the main harbour in busy summer months, while in winter, this beach is only accessible with a private motorboat or sailing boat. There are no facilities on this beach; it has been conserved as a natural beauty. It gives you a chance to spend the whole day swimming, snorkelling, or organizing a barbeque on the pebble stones. Its waters are super clean, and transparent. There are fewer waves also on this side of this island.

23. BEST BEACH TO MEET YOUNG LOCALS

If you would like to meet young locals, you should head to the "Cave" or "Spillia" rocks. It is not really a beach, there are actually rocks, with steps going down in deep sea. Only 5 minutes walk from the main harbour, this is the main meet-up spot for the local youth. In full summer, there is also a "beach bar" called "Spillia", selling light snacks, iced coffees and

>TOURIST

cocktails. This place is not recommended for young children, as it is a deep water diving in swim place. You can dive from the rocks, but always look at the locals first, and if in doubt, ask them about the best spots to dive.

For a safer location, you can head to Kamini beach, with its bar "Castello". After walking around 20 minutes from the main village, on your left, you will reach Kamini harbour and pebble beach. This became an organized beach in 2014, with sun beds, coffee shop, but the local youth did not stop meeting there, for a beach volley game, or just a chat. In summer months, there are also music events, or birthday parties held in Castello restaurant for youngsters.

Finally, you can also try to blend with local youth at Hydronetta rocks, and beach bar. They gather mostly in the afternoons, or for Full moon party, with night swimming and skinny dips! This is part of a tradition in Hydra.

24. BEST BEACH FOR OLDER PEOPLE

Older people in Hydra are used to harsh environment, and going around by foot. They are quite in shape, and many of them start swimming early in the season, as early as March or April. Greek older locals will usually go swimming early morning, before the sunrises, or at sunset. They tend to avoid the hot afternoon hours, and the direct light of the sun.

You will witness also the fact that they stay at least 40 minutes in the water, and do water aerobics in the sea. It is a local saying that the sea helps a lot with rheumatism, and bone pains.

If you visit Hydra in winter, you may still find local older people, swimming. They are called " the winter swimmers", and even stormy waves do not deter them from entering the sea, at Spillia. e

25. GO SCUBA DIVING

http://www.hydra.com.gr/diving-center/

Iannis and Akis will take you on their private boat, for the unique diving experience in Hydra. Please note that private Scuba Diving is not allowed, due to many antiquities under water. Some maritime areas around Hydra are protected. Their office can be found behind the shop called Zoe, facing the harbour, 3rd street from the right. You may contact them before arriving on the island to book an appointment, or ask your hotel reception.

26. SUNSET CRUISE

"Greece is a good place to look at the moon, isn't it"

The poem "Days of Kindness" by Leonard Cohen inspired a few locals on Hydra to launch a "sunset cruise" on a small motorboat. The boat takes no more than 15 people, and you can enjoy a refreshing ride along the coast of the island, while admiring the sunset. You can also try some of the family-owned business 's cocktails! It will offer you a night of fun that you can remember for a long time.

https://www.gnghydracruises.gr

27. FEEL THE NOSTALGIC ATMOSPHERE

Hydra, was so famous in the 1970s with the likes of Onassis, Kennedy's, Elizabeth Taylor, Melina Mercouri, The Beatles visiting during the summer months. While the old "Lagoudera" where they would met has long closed, locals still talk about it, and the building itself was renovated in 2010, opening under the name of Omilos. It still gathers Greek maritime tycoons today, at times of festivals, or celebrations. For example, if you visit on the last weekend of June, to celebrate the victory of the Admiral Miaoulis against Turkish invaders, or for Easter celebrations.

The nostalgic atmosphere is everywhere to remember, with older people telling you tales of Sophia Loren living on Hydra for six months to shoot the movie "Boy and the Dolphin" in 1956. It is also still so present with Leonard Cohen's fans, walking up the steps of "Donkey shit land lane" to find the house he bought in the 1960s.

>TOURIST

28. ORTHODOX EASTER IN HYDRA

Easter is the most important religious celebration in Greece, and in Hydra, it takes a wonderful form: during the week preceding Easter Sunday, relatives of locals start arriving from far away, from the States, Canada, England. Families gather during the week, preparing the traditional ingredients, such as red tinted eggs, candles, and attending the church services every night. On Easter Friday, several processions take place, including the famous one in Kamini harbour, where local men carry the "Epitaphio" into the sea water. Huge crowds travel to Hydra to witness this local tradition. Finally on Easter Saturday night, the "sacred light" reaches Hydra, by sea taxi, directly from Athens airport, and Jerusalem. It is transported to the main church where priests declare "Christos Anesti" Christ is reborn. Following this announcement, crowds rejoice, and go fo a late night diner in local taverns, to eat the traditional Easter soup, made with liver and herbs.

Easter Sunday is a celebration around the island, every house has a barbecue or a roast going on, with dancing, music, family gatherings.

Finally on Easter Monday, celebrations come to an end with the "burning of Juda", and fireworks.

29. INDEPENDENCE DAY IN HYDRA

On March 25th, every year, school children and navy police parade in every town of Greece to celebrate the Independence against Turkish invasion, in 1821. This is a major event everywhere in Greece, but in particular in the islands, including Hydra, where locals gather on this occasion to see the village children wearing the traditional costume. The best student is the one holding the Greek flag, at the front of the parade. Sometimes, a military ship comes to shore, with the musical band playing the national anthem.

If you are visiting Hydra on this day, you can hear the canons fired at 8 am in the morning, then the church bells, and at 11 am the parade comes to life.

>TOURIST

30. MIAOULIS FESTIVAL

Another major event for Hydra is the Miaoulis Festival, which takes place on the last weekend of June, every year. It commemorates the Independence War against Turkey, and the victory of Admiral Miaoulis against the Turkish Navy in 1821. The show starts on the Saturday evening, and is best viewed from "Spillia". It is a naval reconstitution of the battle, with explosion of a replica ship, and fireworks A music concert follows, and during the whole week, many dance and musical events take place. It is a wonderful time of the year to visit Hydra, as temperatures are still bearable, and crowds are mostly Greek.

31. CARNIVAL SEASON IN HYDRA

At the end of the winter months, Carnival season is the first gathering of the year. In Hydra, locals prepare their costumes long in advance, and the parade gathers in the Botsis Square, on Sunday before Clean Monday The parade is a mix of young and older locals, tourists, and Greek visitors from Athens. It goes up to Donkey Shit Lane to Kamini Harbour, and ends up on the harbour side. The Mayor office usually organizes a music concert, with "laiki" (village type) music singer. Dancing goes on long at night! It is a fun time to be in the island, as there are barely any tourists, and you would have more chances to experience the real way of life of Hydra.

Following carnival day is Clean Monday: on this day, it is a tradition to eat specific foods, such as olives, halva paste, smoked fish, and to go to Vlychos village, to fly kites.

32. ZOURVA MONASTERY CELEBRATIONS

Panagia Zourva is a monastery located on one end of the island, which is accessed by sea taxi and 645 steps, or through a horse-riding path that takes a few hours. Every year, locals gather the evening prior to its name day, or early morning on September 8th. They cook and spend the day together at the Monastery. You are welcome to assist as well, if you are on the island at this time of year. You can either board one of the shuttle boats going there on this occasion, or book a private sea taxi to take you there and bring you back.

>TOURIST

33. CLIMB TO THE TOP OF MOUNT EROS

One of the most popular hikes in Hydra is to go up to Profit Ilias Monastery and continue on to the Mount Eros, the highest point of the island. Panoramic views reward all who climbed. If you are not fit enough to walk up, you can also decide to go with a horse, and your own personal guide. A well-known guide is Harriet and her horses: British Born, Hydra educated, Harriet speaks both English and Greek, and she has received hundreds of positive feedbacks on her horse trips. Other horse owners can also arrange trips to the top, and you may be able to negotiate a good price, if you are going as a group of 6 or more. Some tourists like to see the sunset from Mr Eros, but sunrise is also a favourite.

Should you decide to go by foot, you can find some detailed GPS maps, at the local newspaper agency.

34. DRESS CODE

Yes, we are in Greece, so in summer, most days, we would walk around with light cotton clothes, however, Hydra has a classy look at night. You may want to take with you more formal clothes (depending on the season) to visit one of the top restaurants. Similarly, if you are visiting during one of the religious festivals, you would rather wear formal clothes, than shorts and flip flops. Nowadays, tourists tend to walk around in swimsuits, but locals do not.

How about top less and nudism? Well, rumour has it that in the 1980s, the clergy did not agree too much with these, however, nowadays, top less is a pretty common sight There are still no nudist beach as such.

A main point to remember is to bring the right pair of shoes, suitable for Hydra cobbled lanes. The stones tend to get very slippery, with rain or sun, so it is crucial you bring steady, non-slippery soles shoes with you. If you intend to go swimming, it is also wise to bring plastic swim shoes, to avoid sea urchins,

>TOURIST

35. TAKE A GREEK LANGUAGE COURSE

The Hydra Language School started offering Modern Greek lessons, during the summer, in groups or for individuals. There are also a few locals keen on teaching you Greek should you decide to take it on. Tuitions are held from July, on a weekly basis, and tuition fees are given to a charity for education. Teachers are locals, and they do also speak English, sometimes French or Italian.

36. LISTEN TO GREEK MUSIC THROUGH SUMMER

Summer is the busiest season on Hydra Island. Many Greeks visit from Athens, or come to visit family here. It is an opportunity for many outdoors concerts, with pop or classic Greek singers, visiting. In 2018 for example, famous names as Glykeria, or Melina Aslanidou visited the island for exciting nights of music.

Hydra is also famous for its chamber music festival, which takes place every year in August. Most musical events take place in June or August. So if you are into music, and dance, these are the best months to visit Hydra!

37. LISTEN TO BOUZOUKI LIVE MUSIC

Bouzouki is the local Greek music instrument, between a guitar and a lyre. Many locals play this instrument, usually learning from father to son, or through a local teacher. A couple of traditional taverns have them play, not only in the summer, but also for local traditional events, such as carnival, Tchikno pempdi, clean Monday, Easter Sunday, or specific name days. You might meet "Fanassis", "Dimitri" or "Giorgos", while you travel to Hydra.

38. EXPERIENCE THE REBETIKO FESTIVAL

Every year, in October, the Rebetiko Music Festival takes place in Hydra. Rebetiko is a specific form of traditional music, with bouzouki, baglama (small bouzouki). The musicians gather informally in a few taverns, and one night formally at the Douskos Tavern. "Xeri Elia". Back in the 1950s, Rebetiko music had been forbidden, as some wordings and musician's attitudes were not welcomed by politics. However, nowadays, Rebetiko is fully legal, and part of the Greek cultural heritage. If you listen to the informal gathering music, you can just have a bite in one of the taverns. However, if you decide to join the formal event, on Saturday night, you will need to book in advance, and it is a set menu for everyone.

39. JOIN LEONARD COHEN'S FANS

While Leonard Cohen's House now belongs to his children, Adam and Lorca, and his grandson, tourists make the pilgrimage to see the grey door, at the top of the "Donkey Shit Lane" as the locals call it. More than 400 steps to get there, a lane that used to be filled with donkeys carrying merchandises to the upper houses. The house does not have any specific signs, but sometimes a few fresh flowers or a note left by a music lover.

On Hydra, both locals and international fans collected funds to build a "Leonard Cohen" Bench. In 2017, the municipality installed the bench on the paved road to Kamini village. It overlooks the sea, in a beautiful location, and sometimes is a meeting point for friends.

If you still want more, you can join the Leonard Cohen's Informal Festival held in June, every two years.

More than a 150 people gather form around the world: all the way from Australia, Ireland, Norway, or Canada, to sing along, and remember the poet, writer, artist, who composed "Bird on a Wire " in Hydra. These fans became friends to locals, and are now part of the island's life in the month of June. Why not join them?

40. LOCAL FAVOURITE FOODS TO TRY

Most traditional Greek foods are available all around Greece. In Hydra, specific local delicacies include:

"Barbounia": Red mullet fish: there are specific seasons that this fish can be caught. Many Athenians pay a high price to taste the local fresh fishes in local taverns. To watch the fishermen sell their products, you need to wake up early, and be at the harbour side

>TOURIST

by the latest 8.30am. A few wooden caiquis gather near the Alpha Bank corner, and locals come to choose the fish they prefer. Prices are high, as fish is not as abundant as it used to be.

"Octopothakia": Octopus in salad, or grilled, which are caught locally. Young children start fishing early in Hydra, on the harbour side, and later on, with small boats, or on the rocks around.

Fava: a traditional yellow beans purée, served with local lemon juice, and onions. It is a heavy dish, suitable for vegans.

"Horta": the healthy greens collected from the mountains, and traditionally served with seafood dishes, with a lemon juice.

"Manitaria": mushrooms (wild
In the fall, many locals, including the current mayor of the island, go to pick wild mushrooms. Depending on the amount of rain the island had that year, there could be various types of mushrooms available. A few older people know well how to differentiate the poisonous types.

41. LOCAL NIGHTLIFE

There are five major hangouts for locals of all ages at night. Hydra is an island without major clubs or discos, as you would find on Mykonos or Santorin. There are no loud music club, nor beach discos. However these five places are lively and local:

- Pirate Bar: late night cocktails, DJ, some dancing
- Papagalos Bar: outdoor and indoor seating, cocktails, friendly service
- Hydronetta: organizes Full moon parties, Get wet parties
- Amalour Bar: the oldest bar in town, famous with all
- Omilos DJs: the latest addition to the nightlife scene, it brings DJs to town, during the summer months only.

>TOURIST

42. ST CONSTANTINE'S FESTIVAL

This is the Saint patron of Hydra Island. One of the most important Orthodox celebrations takes place in fall: the Ayios Konstandinos Festival. It is held in November, and locals and priests gather at the Church.

The celebrations go on for two days, with a procession from the top of the hill to the cathedral on the port. Many Hydra locals named "Constantine's" or "Kostas" have their name day celebrated on this occasion.

Costumes of the priests and the beauty of the icons make it a special occasion, even if you are not Orthodox yourself.

43. HOW MUCH TO TIP

Tipping in Greece, and in Hydra, is left to one's will. However, I would say that 10% if a good amount to consider, if you were pleased with the service. Service in Hydra is usually very friendly, and as it is a very small place, the waiters, or shop owners will recognize you easily from one day to the next, but also from one year to the next. Many visitors have been coming for more than 10 years, and tipping is one extra way to show their appreciation. Keep in mind also that Greek salaries are rather low, compared to other European countries. A waiter gains on average 700 euros per month.

44. BITES AND OTHER ISSUES

On Hydra, as well as in Greece in general, you may find bees and mosquitoes. There have not been any cases of the Nile disease on Hydra, but you may want to take the regular precautions, with spray or long sleeves, if you are particularly fair-skinned.

Sea Urchins are the most common type of bites, in the sea. They are very common all around the island, and you may not always see them through the waters. It is best to carry a pair of light plastic shoes, to wear when you swim in Avlaki, Kamini, Bisti, or Plakes, Vlychos.

Only in Mandraki Beach Resort, local staff cleaned up the waters, and it is safe enough to walk bare foot in the sea.

Snakes are common on Hydra: both vipers and a brown type of mountain snake. It may sound scary, but actually, in the years I have lived here, I have never heard of anyone being bitten by a snake. Sure, I have seen many of them: on the side of the roads during the summer, in my mountain garden, but they usually leave much faster than you would expect, and they do not tend to attack. If you are planning to hike in the mountains during summer months, it is best to wear closed boots, and perhaps trousers. If you see a snake from a distance, tap your feet on the road, till it hears you.

There is a small hospital, dispensary-like, where nurses and a doctor can attend to emergencies, should an incident occur.

45. SAFETY OR HEALTH CONCERNS

Mobile phone may not be operating on the entire island. Some areas may be out of coverage. If you are planning to hike alone, in the mountains, please let someone know at your hotel, or guesthouse. Take always plenty of water (1 bottle at least), sun protection, and jumper. If you find yourself facing cattle dogs, stay calm; their owner is not far and shall recall them.

During fall, hunting season is on, and hunters are shooting in various hills around the island. Ask locals if you can still hike the tracks you wish.

Please note that although there is a desalting water plant, most people still drink bottled water.

At night, keep safe as you would if you are travelling alone. It is generally safe to walk alone on small dark lanes, but it may come handy to have an electric torch with you.

Finally, if you are visiting Hydra during the raining months (October, November, February, March) please keep in mind that rain can start suddenly, with huge volume of water coming down from the mountain onto the streets. In 2016, water levels raised up to shoulder level. In this event, please stay put in a restaurant, coffee shop, or elevated point. Do not try to walk the streets if you witness water levels going up fast.

Major heath emergencies need to be evacuated through helicopter, therefore it is best to subscribe to strong travel insurance, before you arrive in Greece.

>TOURIST

46. IT'S ALL-GREEK TO ME

Modern Greek is slightly different than Ancient Greek, and the alphabet may surprise you at first. However, a few greetings words are easy to remember:

Kalimera (pronounce Kalee-Mayra): good morning to use until around 1pm

Kalispera (pronounce Kalee Spayra): good evening, to use from 3pm to 10pm

Kalinikta: (pronounce Kalee Nikta): good night

Yassou/ Yassas: Good Day!

Efkaristo: Thank you

Parakalo: Please or You are welcomed

Poso kanei? How much is it?

Pou einai? Where is

Me lene (Carolina): My name is (Caroline)

Do not worry though, most locals speak if not only English, also French, Italian, Japanese and sometimes Arabic.

47. TIME FOR SHOPPING

There are many shops, mostly located around the harbour side, in the main village, and the parallels streets from the port. Local crafts include paintings, ceramics, or hand woven bags and carpets from the monasteries. Watch out for labels, to make sure it is locally made. Leather crafts are also popular on Hydra, while created on another island, Crete

If you fancy delicacies, you can visit two small shops selling local honey, spices, and sweets. One is called "Filotimo" "Greek proud".

Finally, if you have a higher budget, there are also a few designer jewellery shops, such as Elena Votsi. Born on Hydra, the designer works with Ralph Lauren, and created the Olympic medals for Athens Olympics in 2004. Check out also Zoe's, Greco's Gold, or Marilena Maramenou.

For crafts, you can always stop and say hello to Carolina's arts & crafts!

48. BEFORE YOU LEAVE

Do not forget to visit the local post office! They have special collectors stamps, with Melina Mercouri, for example. You can post any package or express mail for this local office, and your mail will reach your destination worldwide, usually within 4 to 5 days!

49. TAKE A BOAT TO THE NEXT ISLAND

From Hydra, it is easy to navigate in the Argo-Saronic Gulf, to explore other islands close by. For example, if you board the Flying Cat again, you can get easily to Spetses, or Poros Islands, within 45 minutes.

Another option it to board the local motorboat of "Christos", which goes to Hermione across the Peloponnese, and from there, explore Nafplion, Epidaurus or Galatas.

From Hydra, you can also board a sailing boat flotilla, a so-called chartered sailing boat, which will take you to the Cyclades, for a week.

Finally, why not join a local captain, such Panayiotis Miras, on his wooden boat: he has travelled as far as Egypt with his wooden caiqui, but he is ready to take around the gulf, for a reasonable price.

50. BUY A HOUSE

Many visitors who came as tourists never left: they ended up buying a house, 50 years ago, 2 years ago…."Hydra never loses its value" is a local saying. There are a couple of real estate agents on the island, though most business is through online sites. If you have the budget and are serious about buying a place here, ask one of the older gentlemen at a coffee shop, and look for "Christos", "Kelsey" or "Tracey". Alternatively, check their sites, such as Hydra Direct, Hydra Dream Houses.

>TOURIST

TOP REASONS TO BOOK THIS TRIP

Hydra is Out of this world: It is One of A Kind

Tranquillity: Hydra is one of the few places on earth car-free

Beach, food, history: It has it all, and it is close to Athens.

>TOURIST

OTHER RESOURCES:

Links to travel websites or maps of the area.

http://hydrawalkingtours.com/short-walk/
https://www.hydradirect.com
https://www.theguardian.com/travel/2016/dec/04/hydra-greece-leonard-cohen
https://thepiratebar.gr
http://omilos-hydra.com/omilos.html
https://www.greeka.com/saronic/hydra/hydra-festivals/hydra-rebetiko-conference.htm
http://www.fourseasonshydra.gr
http://www.ippokampos.com
https://www.orloff.gr
https://weddinghydra.com
https://hydratourism.gr
http://fonitisydras.com/en/item/2709-hydra-school-summer-lessons-for-aspiring-greek-speakers

BONUS TIPS

50 THINGS TO KNOW ABOUT PACKING LIGHT FOR TRAVEL

PACK THE RIGHT WAY EVERY TIME

AUTHOR: MANIDIPA BHATTACHARYYA

First Published in 2015 by Dr. Lisa Rusczyk. Copyright 2015. All Rights Reserved. No part of this publication may be reproduced, including scanning and photocopying, or distributed in any form or by any means, electronic or mechanical, or stored in a database or retrieval system without prior written permission from the publisher.

Disclaimer: The publisher has put forth an effort in preparing and arranging this book. The information provided herein by the author is provided "as is". Use this information at your own risk. The publisher is not a licensed doctor. Consult your doctor before engaging in any medical activities. The publisher and author disclaim any liabilities for any loss of profit or commercial or personal damages resulting from the information contained in this book.

Edited by Melanie Howthorne

ABOUT THE AUTHOR

Manidipa Bhattacharyya is a creative writer and editor, with an education in English literature and Linguistics. After working in the IT industry for seven long years she decided to call it quits and follow her heart instead. Manidipa has been ghost writing, editing, proof reading and doing secondary research services for many story tellers and article writers for about three years. She stays in Kolkata, India with her husband and a busy two year old. In her own time Manidipa enjoys travelling, photography and writing flash fiction.

Manidipa believes in travelling light and never carries anything that she couldn't haul herself on a trip. However, travelling with her child changed the scenario. She seemed to carry the entire world with her for the baby on the first two trips. But good sense prevailed and she is again working her way to becoming a light traveler, this time with a kid.

INTRODUCTION

*He who would travel happily
must travel light.*

-Antoine de Saint-Exupéry

Travel takes you to different places from seas and mountains to deserts and much more. In your travels you get to interact with different people and their cultures. You will, however, enjoy the sights and interact positively with these new people even more, if you are travelling light.

When you travel light your mind can be free from worry about your belongings. You do not have to spend precious vacation time waiting for your luggage to arrive after a long flight. There is be no chance of your bags going missing and the best part is that you need not pay a fee for checked baggage.

People who have mastered this art of packing light will root for you to take only one carry-on, wherever you go. However, many people can find it really hard to pack light. More so if you are travelling with children. Differentiating between "must have" and "just in case" items is the starting point. There will be ample shopping avenues at your destination which are just waiting to be explored.

This book will show you 'packing' in a new 'light' – pun intended – and help you to embrace light packing practices for all of your future travels.

Off to packing!

DEDICATION

I dedicate this book to all the travel buffs that I know, who have given me great insights into the contents of their backpacks.

THE RIGHT TRAVEL GEAR

1. CHOOSE YOUR TRAVEL GEAR CAREFULLY

While selecting your travel gear, pick items that are light weight, durable and most importantly, easy to carry. There are cases with wheels so you can drag them along – these are usually on the heavy side because of the trolley. Alternatively a backpack that you can carry comfortably on your back, or even a duffel bag that you can carry easily by hand or sling across your body are also great options. Whatever you choose, one thing to keep in mind is that the luggage itself should not weigh a ton, this will give you the flexibility to bring along one extra pair of shoes if you so desire.

2. CARRY THE MINIMUM NUMBER OF BAGS

Selecting light weight luggage is not everything. You need to restrict the number of bags you carry as well. One carry-on size bag is ideal for light travel. Most carriers allow one cabin baggage plus one purse, handbag or camera bag as long as it slides under the seat in front. So technically, you can carry two items of luggage without checking them in.

3. PACK ONE EXTRA BAG

Always pack one extra empty bag along with your essential items. This could be a very light weight duffel bag or even a sturdy tote bag which takes up minimal space. In the event that you end up buying a lot of souvenirs, you already have a handy bag to stuff all that into and do not have to spend time hunting for an appropriate bag.

> *I'm very strict with my packing and have everything in its right place. I never change a rule. I hardly use anything in the hotel room. I wheel my own wardrobe in and that's it.*
>
> Charlie Watts

CLOTHES & ACCESSORIES

4. PLAN AHEAD

Figure out in advance what you plan to do on your trip. That will help you to pick that one dress you need for the occasion. If you are going to attend a wedding then you have to carry formal wear. If not, you can ditch the gown for something lighter that will be comfortable during long walks or on the beach.

5. WEAR THAT JACKET

Remember that wearing items will not add extra luggage for your air travel. So wear that bulky jacket that you plan to carry for your trip. This saves space and can also help keep you warm during the chilly flight.

6. MIX AND MATCH

Carry clothes that can be interchangeably used to reinvent your look. Find one top that goes well with a couple of pairs of pants or skirts. Use tops, shirts and jackets wisely along with other accessories like a scarf or a stole to create a new look.

7. CHOOSE YOUR FABRIC WISELY

Stuffing clothes in cramped bags definitely takes its toll which results in wrinkles. It is best to carry wrinkle free, synthetic clothes or merino tops. This will eliminate the need for that small iron you usually bring along.

8. DITCH CLOTHES PACK UNDERWEAR

Pack more underwear and socks. These are the things that will give you a fresh feel even if you do not get a chance to wear fresh clothes. Moreover these are easy to wash and can be dried inside the hotel room itself.

9. CHOOSE DARK OVER LIGHT

While picking your clothes choose dark coloured ones. They are easy to colour coordinate and can last longer before needing a wash. Accidental food spills and dirt from the road are less visible on darker clothes.

10. WEAR YOUR JEANS

Take only one pair of Jeans with you, which you should wear on the flight. Remember to pick a pair that can be worn for sightseeing trips and is equally eloquent for dinner. You can add variety by adding light weight cargoes and chinos.

11. CARRY SMART ACCESSORIES

The right accessory can give you a fresh look even with the same old dress. An intelligent neck-piece, a couple of bright scarves, stoles or a sarong can be used in a number of ways to add variety to your clothing. These light weight beauties can double up as a nursing cover, a light blanket, beach wear, a modesty cover for visiting places of worship, and also makes for an enthralling game of peek-a-boo.

12. LEARN TO FOLD YOUR GARMENTS

Seasoned travellers all swear by rolling their clothes for compact and wrinkle free packing. Bundle packing, where you roll the clothes around a central object as if tying it up, is also a popular method of compact and wrinkle free packing. Stacking folded clothes one on top of another is a big no-no as it makes creases extreme and they are difficult to get rid of without ironing.

13. WASH YOUR DIRTY LAUNDRY

One of the ways to avoid carrying loads of clothes is to wash the clothes you carry. At some places you might get to use the laundry services or a Laundromat but if you are in a pinch, best solution is to wash them yourself. If that is the plan then carrying quick drying clothes is highly recommended, which most often also happen to be the wrinkle free variety.

14. LEAVE THOSE TOWELS BEHIND

Regular towels take up a lot of space, are heavy and take ages to dry out. If you are staying at hotels they will provide you with towels anyway. If you are travelling to a remote place, where the availability of towels look doubtful, carry a light weight travel towel of viscose material to do the job.

15. USE A COMPRESSION BAG

Compression bags are getting lots of recommendation now days from regular travellers. These are useful for saving space in your luggage when you have to pack bulky dresses. While packing for the return trip, get help from the hotel staff to arrange a vacuum cleaner.

FOOTWEAR

16. PUT ON YOUR HIKING BOOTS

If you have plans to go hiking or trekking during your trip, you will need those bulky hiking boots. The best way to carry them is to wear them on flight to save space and luggage weight. You can remove the boots once inside and be comfortable in your socks.

17. PICKING THE RIGHT SHOES

Shoes are often the bulkiest items, along with being the dainty if you are a female. They need care and take up a lot of space in your luggage. It is advisable therefore to pick shoes very carefully. If you plan to do a lot of walking and site seeing, then wearing a pair of comfortable walking shoes are a must. For more formal occasions you can carry durable, light weight flats which will not take up much space.

18. STUFF SHOES

If you happen to pack a pair of shoes, ensure you utilize their hollow insides. Tuck small items like rolled up socks or belts to save space. They will also be easy to find.

\>TOURIST

TOILETRIES

19. STASHING TOILETRIES

Carry only absolute necessities. Airline rules dictate that for one carry-on bag, liquids and gels must be in 3.4 ounce (100ml) bottles or less, and must be packed in a one quart zip-lock bag. If you are planning to stay in a hotel, the basic things will be provided for you. It's best is to buy the rest from the local market at your destination.

20. TAKE ALONG TAMPONS

Tampons are a hard to find item in a lot of countries. Figure out how many you need and pack accordingly. For longer stays you can buy them online and have them delivered to where you are staying.

21. GET PAMPERED BEFORE YOU TRAVEL

Some avid travellers suggest getting a pedicure and manicure just the day before travelling. This not only gives you a well kept look, you also save the trouble of packing nail polish. Remember, every little bit of weight reduced adds up.

ELECTRONICS

22. LUGGING ALONG ELECTRONICS

Electronics have a large role to play in our lives today. Most of us cannot imagine our lives away from our phones, laptops or tablets. However while travelling, one must consider the amount of weight these electronics add to our luggage. Thankfully smart phones come along with all the essentials tools like a camera, email access, picture editing tools and more. They are smart to the point of eliminating the need to carry multiple gadgets. Choose a smart phone that suits all your requirements and travel with the world in your palms or pocket.

23. REDUCE THE NUMBER OF CHARGERS

If you do travel with multiple electronic devices, you will have to bear the additional burden of carrying all their chargers too. Check if a single charger can be used for multiple devices. You might also consider investing in a pocket charger. These small devices support multiple devices while keeping you charged on the go.

24. TRAVEL FRIENDLY APPS

Along with smart phones come numerous apps, which are immensely helpful in our travels. You name it and you have an app for it at hand – take pictures, sharing with friends and family, torch to light dark roads, maps, checking flight/train times, find hotels and many other things. Use these smart alternatives to traditional items like books to eliminate weight and save space.

> *I get ideas about what's essential
> when packing my suitcase.*

-Diane von Furstenberg

TRAVELLING WITH KIDS

25. BRING ALONG THE STROLLER

Kids might enjoy walking for a while but they soon tire out and a stroller is the just the right thing for them to rest in while you continue your tour. Strollers also double duty as a luggage carrier and shopping bag holder. Remember to pick a light weight, easy to handle brand of stroller. Better yet, find out in advance if you can rent a stroller at your destination.

26. BRING ONLY ENOUGH DIAPERS FOR YOUR TRIP

Diapers take up a lot of space and add to the weight of your luggage. Therefore it is advisable to carry just enough diapers to last through the trip and a few for afterwards, till you buy fresh stock at your destination. Unless of course you are travelling to a really remote area, in which case you have no choice but to carry the load. Otherwise diapers are something you will find pretty easily.

27. TAKE ONLY A COUPLE OF TOYS

Children are easily attracted by new things in their environment. While travelling they will find numerous 'new' objects to scrutinize and play with. Packing just one favorite toy is enough, or if there is no favorite toy leave out all of them in favor of stories or imaginary games.

28. CARRY KID FRIENDLY SNACKS

Create a small snack counter in your bag to store away quick bites for those sudden hunger pangs. Depending on the child's age this could include chocolates, raisins, dry fruits, granola bars or biscuits. Also keep a bottle of water handy for your little one.

These things do not add much weight and can be adjusted in a handbag or knapsack.

29. GAMES TO CARRY

Create some travel specific, imaginary games if you have slightly grown up children, like spot the attractions. Keep a coloring book and colors handy for in-flight or hotel time. Apps on your smart phone can keep the children engaged with cartoons and story books. Older children are often entertained by games available on phones or tablets. This cuts the weight of luggage down while keeping the kids entertained.

30. LET THE KIDS CARRY THEIR LOAD

A good thing is to start early sharing of responsibilities. Let your child pick a bag of his or her choice and pack it themselves. Keep tabs on what they are stuffing in their bags by asking if they will be using that item on the trip. It could start out being just an entertainment bag initially but with growing years they will learn to sort the useful from the superfluous. Children as little as four can maneuver a small trolley suitcase like a pro- their experience in pull along toys credit. If you are worried that you may be pulling it for them, you may want to start with a backpack.

31. DECIDE ON LOCATION FOR CHILDREN TO SLEEP

While on a trip you might not always get a crib at your destination, and carrying one will make life all the more difficult. Instead call ahead to see if there are any cribs or roll out beds for children. You may even put blankets on the floor. Weave them a story about camping and they will gladly sleep without any trouble.

32. GET BABY PRODUCTS DELIVERED AT YOUR DESTINATION

If you are absolutely paranoid about not getting your favourite variety of diaper or brand of baby food, check out online stores like amazon.com for services in your destination city. You can buy things online ahead of your travel and get them delivered to your hotel upon arrival.

33. FEEDING NEEDS OF YOUR INFANTS

If you are travelling with a breastfed infant, you save the trouble of carrying bottles and bottle sanitization kits. For special food, or medications, you may need to call ahead to make sure you have a refrigerator where you are staying.

34. FEEDING NEEDS OF YOUR TODDLER

With the progression from infancy to toddler, their dietary requirements too evolve. You will have to pack some snacks for travelling time. Fresh fruits and vegetables can be purchased at your destination. Most of the cities you travel to in whichever part of the world, will have baby food products and formulas, available at the local drug-store or the supermarket.

35. PICKING CLOTHES FOR YOUR BABY

Contrary to popular belief, babies can do without many changes of clothes. At the most pack 2 outfits per day. Pack mix and match type clothes for your little one as well. Pick things which are comfortable to wear and quick to dry.

36. SELECTING SHOES FOR YOUR BABY

Like outfits, kids can make do with two pairs of comfortable shoes. If you can get some water resistant shoes it will be best. To expedite drying wet shoes, you can stuff newspaper in them then wrap them with newspaper and leave them to dry overnight.

37. KEEP ONE CHANGE OF CLOTHES HANDY

Travelling with kids can be tricky. Keep a change of clothes for the kids and mum handy in your purse or tote bag. This takes a bit of space in your hand luggage but comes extremely handy in case there are any accidents or spills.

38. LEAVE BEHIND BABY ACCESSORIES

Baby accessories like their bed, bath tub, car seat, crib etc. should be left at home. Many hotels provide a crib on request, while car seats can be borrowed from friends or rented. Babies can be given a bath in the hotel sink or even in the adult bath tub with a little bit of water. If you bring a few bath toys, they can be used in the bath, pool, and out of water. They can also be sanitized easily in the sink.

39. CARRY A SMALL LOAD OF PLASTIC BAGS

With children around there are chances of a number of soiled clothes and diapers. These plastic bags help to sort the dirt from the clean inside your big bag.

>TOURIST

These are very light weight and come in handy to other carry stuff as well at times.

PACK WITH A PURPOSE

40. PACKING FOR BUSINESS TRIPS

One neutral-colored suit should suffice. It can be paired with different shirts, ties and accessories for different occasions. One pair of black suit pants could be worn with a matching jacket for the office or with a snazzy top for dinner.

41. PACKING FOR A CRUISE

Most cruises have formal dinners, and that formal dress usually takes up a lot of space. However you might find a tuxedo to rent. For women, a short black dress with multiple accessory options will do the trick.

42. PACKING FOR A LONG TRIP OVER DIFFERENT CLIMATES

The secret packing mantra for travel over multiple climates is layering. Layering traps air around your body creating insulation against the cold. The same light t-shirt that is comfortable in a warmer climate can be the innermost layer in a colder climate.

REDUCE SOME MORE WEIGHT

43. LEAVE PRECIOUS THINGS AT HOME

Things that you would hate to lose or get damaged leave them at home. Precious jewelry, expensive gadgets or dresses, could be anything. You will not require these on your trip. Leave them at home and spare the load on your mind.

44. SEND SOUVENIRS BY MAIL

If you have spent all your money on purchasing souvenirs, carrying them back in the same bag that you brought along would be difficult. Either pack everything in another bag and check it in the airport or get everything shipped to your home. Use an international carrier for a secure transit, but this could be more expensive than the checking fees at the airport.

45. AVOID CARRYING BOOKS

Books equal to weight. There are many reading apps which you can download on your smart phone or tab.

Plus there are gadgets like Kindle and Nook that are thinner and lighter alternatives to your regular book.

CHECK, GET, SET, CHECK AGAIN

46. STRATEGIZE BEFORE PACKING

Create a travel list and prepare all that you think you need to carry along. Keep everything on your bed or floor before packing and then think through once again – do I really need that? Any item that meets this question can be avoided. Remove whatever you don't really need and pack the rest.

47. TEST YOUR LUGGAGE

Once you have fully packed for the trip take a test trip with your luggage. Take your bags and go to town for window shopping for an hour. If you enjoy your hour long trip it is good to go, if not, go home and reduce the load some more. Repeat this test till you hit the right weight.

48. ADD A ROLL OF DUCT TAPE

You might wonder why, when this book has been talking about reducing stuff, we're suddenly asking you to pack something totally unusual. This is because when you have limited supplies, duct tape is immensely helpful for small repairs – a broken bag, leaking zip-lock bag, broken sunglasses, you name it and duct tape can fix it, temporarily.

49. LIST OF ESSENTIAL ITEMS

Even though the emphasis is on packing light, there are things which have to be carried for any trip. Here is our list of essentials:

- Passport/Visa or any other ID
- Any other paper work that might be required on a trip like permits, hotel reservation confirmations etc.
- Medicines – all your prescription medicines and emergency kit, especially if you are travelling with children
- Medical or vaccination records
- Money in foreign currency if travelling to a different country
- Tickets- Email or Message them to your phone

>TOURIST

50. MAKE THE MOST OF YOUR TRIP

Wherever you are going, whatever you hope to do we encourage you to embrace it whole-heartedly. Take in the scenery, the culture and above all, enjoy your time away from home.

On a long journey even a straw weighs heavy.

-Spanish Proverb

\>TOURIST

PACKING AND PLANNING TIPS

A Week before Leaving

- Arrange for someone to take care of pets and water plants.
- Email and Print important Documents.
- Get Visa and vaccines if needed.
- Check for travel warnings.
- Stop mail and newspaper.
- Notify Credit Card companies where you are going.
- Passports and photo identification is up to date.
- Pay bills.
- Copy important items and download travel Apps.
- Start collecting small bills for tips.
- Have post office hold mail while you are away.
- Check weather for the week.
- Car inspected, oil is changed, and tires have the correct pressure.
- Check airline luggage restrictions.
- Download Apps needed for your trip.

Right Before Leaving

- Contact bank and credit cards to tell them your location.
- Clean out refrigerator.
- Empty garbage cans.
- Lock windows.
- Make sure you have the proper identification with you.
- Bring cash for tips.
- Remember travel documents.
- Lock door behind you.
- Remember wallet.
- Unplug items in house and pack chargers.
- Change your thermostat settings.
- Charge electronics, and prepare camera memory cards.

>TOURIST

READ OTHER GREATER THAN A TOURIST BOOKS

Greater Than a Tourist- Geneva Switzerland: 50 Travel Tips from a Local by Amalia Kartika

Greater Than a Tourist- St. Croix US Birgin Islands USA: 50 Travel Tips from a Local by Tracy Birdsall

Greater Than a Tourist- San Juan Puerto Rico: 50 Travel Tips from a Local by Melissa Tait

Greater Than a Tourist – Lake George Area New York USA: 50 Travel Tips from a Local by Janine Hirschklau

Greater Than a Tourist – Monterey California United States: 50 Travel Tips from a Local by Katie Begley

Greater Than a Tourist – Chanai Crete Greece: 50 Travel Tips from a Local by Dimitra Papagrigoraki

Greater Than a Tourist – The Garden Route Western Cape Province South Africa: 50 Travel Tips from a Local by Li-Anne McGregor van Aardt

Greater Than a Tourist – Sevilla Andalusia Spain: 50 Travel Tips from a Local by Gabi Gazon

Children's Book: *Charlie the Cavalier Travels the World* by Lisa Rusczyk

> TOURIST

Visit *Greater Than a Tourist* for Free Travel Tips
http://GreaterThanATourist.com

Sign up for the *Greater Than a Tourist* Newsletter for discount days, new books, and travel information:
http://eepurl.com/cxspyf

Follow us on Facebook for tips, images, and ideas:
https://www.facebook.com/GreaterThanATourist

Follow us on Pinterest for travel tips and ideas:
http://pinterest.com/GreaterThanATourist

Follow us on Instagram for beautiful travel images:
http://Instagram.com/GreaterThanATourist

Follow *Greater Than a Tourist* on Amazon.

> TOURIST

At *Greater Than a Tourist*, we love to share travel tips with you. How did we do? What guidance do you have for how we can give you better advice for your next trip? Please send your feedback to GreaterThanaTourist@gmail.com as we continue to improve the series. We appreciate your constructive feedback. Thank you.

>TOURIST

METRIC CONVERSIONS

TEMPERATURE

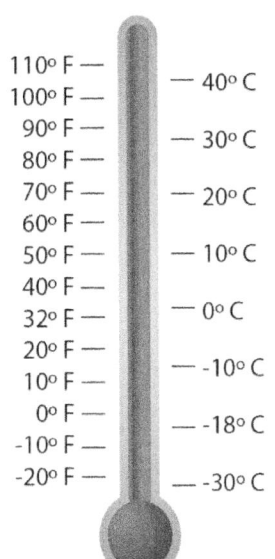

110° F — 40° C
100° F
90° F — 30° C
80° F
70° F — 20° C
60° F
50° F — 10° C
40° F
32° F — 0° C
20° F
10° F — -10° C
0° F — -18° C
-10° F
-20° F — -30° C

To convert F to C:

Subtract 32, and then multiply by 5/9 or .5555.

To Convert C to F:
Multiply by 1.8 and then add 32.

32F = 0C

LIQUID VOLUME

To Convert:....................Multiply by
U.S. Gallons to Liters................. 3.8
U.S. Liters to Gallons 26
Imperial Gallons to U.S. Gallons 1.2
Imperial Gallons to Liters....... 4.55
Liters to Imperial Gallons 22
1 Liter = .26 U.S. Gallon
1 U.S. Gallon = 3.8 Liters

DISTANCE

To convert ....Multiply by
Inches to Centimeters 2.54
Centimeters to Inches 39
Feet to Meters........................ .3
Meters to Feet 3.28
Yards to Meters 91
Meters to Yards 1.09
Miles to Kilometers 1.61
Kilometers to Miles............ .62
1 Mile = 1.6 km
1 km = .62 Miles

WEIGHT

1 Ounce = .28 Grams
1 Pound = .4555 Kilograms
1 Gram = .04 Ounce
1 Kilogram = 2.2 Pounds

>TOURIST

TRAVEL QUESTIONS

- Do you bring presents home to family or friends after a vacation?
- Do you get motion sick?
- Do you have a favorite billboard?
- Do you know what to do if there is a flat tire?
- Do you like a sun roof open?
- Do you like to eat in the car?
- Do you like to wear sun glasses in the car?
- Do you like toppings on your ice cream?
- Do you use public bathrooms?
- Did you bring your cell phone and does it have power?
- Do you have a form of identification with you?
- Have you ever been pulled over by a cop?
- Have you ever given money to a stranger on a road trip?
- Have you ever taken a road trip with animals?
- Have you ever went on a vacation alone?
- Have you ever run out of gas?

- If you could move to any place in the world, where would it be?
- If you could travel anywhere in the world, where would you travel?
- If you could travel in any vehicle, which one would it be?
- If you had three things to wish for from a magic genie, what would they be?
- If you have a driver's license, how many times did it take you to pass the test?
- What are you the most afraid of on vacation?
- What do you want to get away from the most when you are on vacation?
- What foods smells bad to you?
- What item do you bring on ever trip with you away from home?
- What makes you sleepy?
- What song would you love to hear on the radio when you're cruising on the highway?
- What travel job would you want the least?
- What will you miss most while you are away from home?
- What is something you always wanted to try?

\>TOURIST

- What is the best road side attraction that you ever saw?
- What is the farthest distance you ever biked?
- What is the farthest distance you ever walked?
- What is the weirdest thing you needed to buy while on vacation?
- What is your favorite candy?
- What is your favorite color car?
- What is your favorite family vacation?
- What is your favorite food?
- What is your favorite gas station drink or food?
- What is your favorite license plate design?
- What is your favorite restaurant?
- What is your favorite smell?
- What is your favorite song?
- What is your favorite sound that nature makes?
- What is your favorite thing to bring home from a vacation?
- What is your favorite vacation with friends?
- What is your favorite way to relax?

- Where is the farthest place you ever traveled in a car?
- Where is the farthest place you ever went North, South, East and West?
- Where is your favorite place in the world?
- Who is your favorite singer?
- Who taught you how to drive?
- Who will you miss the most while you are away?
- Who if the first person you will contact when you get to your destination?
- Who brought you on your first vacation?
- Who likes to travel the most in your life?
- Would you rather be hot or cold?
- Would you rather drive above, below, or at the speed limited?
- Would you rather drive on a highway or a back road?
- Would you rather go on a train or a boat?
- Would you rather go to the beach or the woods?

>TOURIST

TRAVEL BUCKET LIST

1.

2.

3.

4.

5.

6.

7.

8.

9.

10.

Printed in Great Britain
by Amazon

15228332R00062